PYRAMIDS

Joyce Filer

OXFORD
UNIVERSITY PRESS

This book is dedicated to Matthew and Jonathan
Smith of Wirral, Cheshire and to my dear friend
Janis, their mum (and Graham)

Grateful thanks to: Stephen Horvath IV for his valuable advice on design;
also to Courteney and Donna Nottage, Alex Bercow and Alice Osbourne.
Thanks to: Claire Thorne for her drawings; Jeffrey Spencer for advice and
comments; to Blokes At Work Productions for photographic work. To Tania
Watkins; Beatriz Waters; the Petrie Museum, London; Rikki Barritt and Ted
for support. Big thanks to my editor Carolyn Jones.

Published in the United States of America by
Oxford University Press, Inc.
198 Madison Avenue
New York, NY 10016-4314
www.oup.com
Oxford is a registered trademark of Oxford University Press, Inc.

Library of Congress Cataloging-in-Publication Data
Filer, Joyce.
  Pyramids / Joyce M. Filer.-- 2nd ed.
    p. cm.
  Previously published as: Pyramids and people of ancient Egypt.
  Includes index.
  ISBN-13: 978-0-19-530521-0 (trade); ISBN-10: 0-19-530521-3 (trade)
  ISBN-13: 978-0-19-530525-8 (library); ISBN-10: 0-19-530525-6 (library)
  1. Pyramids--Egypt--Juvenile literature. I. Filer, Joyce. Pyramids
  and people of ancient Egypt. II. Title.
  DT63.F54 2005
  932--dc22

                        2005017117

Original page design and cover design by Turchini Design
Designed and typeset by Proof Books
Printed by Oriental Press, Dubai

Illustration acknowledgements
Photographs are © the Trustees of the British Museum unless otherwise stated.
Carol Andrews: 14 top right, 15 top right, 19 top right.
Alexandra Bercow: 26 centre right.
Peter Clayton: 3 centre, 9 top centre, 11 top, 15 top left, 16-17 bottom
centre, 19 bottom, 21 bottom left, 23 bottom right, 24 top, 35 top right,
36 bottom, 43 top right, 47 centre left.
Corbis: © Bernard Annebicque /CORBIS SYGMA: 21 bottom right;
© Nigel Francis/CORBIS: front cover, 20-21; © Carmen Redondo/CORBIS 8.
Martin Dexter: 46 top right.
Aidan Dodson: 14 left.
Editions Errance (watercolours Jean-Claude Golvin): 5 top, 10-11 top.
Joyce Filer: 6-7 top centre, 7 right second from top, 7 bottom left, 11
bottom right, 12 bottom, 13 bottom right, 20 bottom left, 23 top right, 25
top, 29 top right, 29 bottom left, 30 bottom, 34 bottom left, 34 bottom
right, 34 centre right, 35 centre right, 37 bottom right, 42 top right, 42
bottom right, 42 background, 45, 46 centre left, 47 top left: 47 centre right.
Werner Forman Archive/Egyptian Museum Cairo: 17 top, 32-33 centre;
Werner Forman Archive: 26 bottom.
Graham Harrison: 4-5, 7 bottom right, 9 top right, 12-13 centre, 22
bottom, 24 bottom, 34 top right.
Lonely Planet Images/Donald C. & Priscilla Alexander Eastman: 3 top, 28
bottom.
Luxor Las Vegas: 46-47 centre.
Stuart MacRae: 46 bottom left.
Marcel Marée: 18 top, 30 top, 31 centre, 37 centre, and typesetting of
hieroglyphs for kings' names on 9, 14, 22, 25, 28, 30, 34, 36, 38.
ML Design: 2 map.
© 2005 Museum of Fine Arts, Boston. King Menkaure and Queen. Egyptian,
Old Kingdom, Dyn. 4, about 2490-2472 B.C. findspot: Egypt. Giza, Menkaure
Valley Temple. Grewacke. H x W x D: 142.2 x 57.1 x 55.2 cm. Harvard
University - Museum of Fine Arts Expedition. 11.1738: 3 bottom, 28 top.
Bob Partridge: 22 centre left, 25 bottom left, 38 bottom.
Delia Pemberton: 27 left.
Petrie Museum of Egyptian Archaeology, University College London: 31 bottom.
By permission of Margaret Drower, from Flinders Petrie: A Life in
Archaeology by Margaret Drower (Victor Gollancz 1983): 37 top right.
© The Oriental Institute Ahmose & Tetisheri Project. Photo: Laura Foos: 39 top.
© Photo RMN - B Hatala: 31 top right.
Ann Searight: 44 bottom left.
From G. Elliot Smith, The Royal Mummies (Catalogue General du Musée du
Caire), (Cairo, 1912): 38 top right.
Steven Snape: 16 top right, 31 background.
Kate Spence: 41 top.
Claire Thorne: drawings on 12, 16, 18, 19, 22, 26, 29, 32, 35, 36, 37, 40, 41.
Derek Welsby: 44 top.

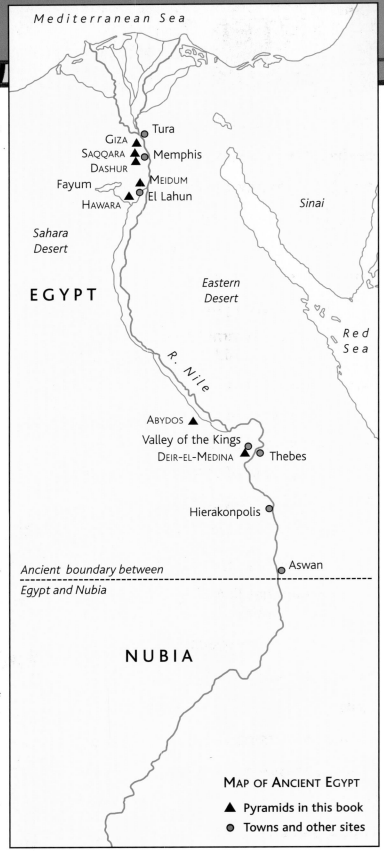

MAP OF ANCIENT EGYPT

▲ Pyramids in this book

● Towns and other sites

Contents

WHAT IS A PYRAMID?

Pyramids are Egypt's oldest and most famous monuments, but what exactly is a pyramid? Why did the Egyptians build them?

The word 'pyramid' describes a building with a very special shape. Egyptian pyramids had four sides and stood on a flat, square base with the sides sloping up to a point.

The Egyptians believed that their king was like a god living on earth. When he died his body was made into a mummy so it would survive for ever. The Egyptians needed a special place for the mummy – a pyramid. The pyramid looked as if its top would reach the sky so it was an excellent place to bury a god-like king.

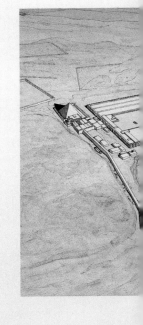

Strength and protection

Why did the ancient Egyptians choose this particular shape? It's a very strong shape. Think of a modern egg-box – it is made of lots of small pyramids which protect the eggs inside. A building in the same shape – if it is built properly – will be very strong. This is what the Egyptians needed to protect the mummy of the king.

The pyramids of Giza.

Egypt has many pyramids. Including all the ones in Nubia (modern Sudan) as well, there are over a hundred. The pyramids at Giza in Egypt are world-famous. The Giza pyramids have stood up for a very long time because their particular shape has made them extremely strong.

This book explores many different pyramids in Egypt. Every single one was built for a special purpose – the burial of the king and his possessions. In places outside Egypt there are other ancient pyramid-shaped buildings, but they were used for different purposes.

Pyramid people

When it was built, an Egyptian pyramid did not stand by itself in the desert. Each pyramid was surrounded by many other buildings. The king might have a palace built near his pyramid. There were temples where the royal mummies were made and houses for the priests who worked in the temples. There were workshops, storerooms and houses for the workers.

It's important to remember the people who were involved with pyramids: the workmen who designed, built and decorated them, and the great kings of Egypt (and their families) who were buried in these wonderful ancient structures.

Four pyramid complexes at Saqqara. The Step Pyramid of Djoser (see page 8) is the largest.

Imhotep was the designer of the first pyramid ever built in Egypt, the Step Pyramid of King Djoser.

BEFORE THE PYRAMIDS

What was it like in Egypt in the time before the Egyptians built pyramids?

About 12,000 years ago the earliest people in Egypt began to live along the banks of the River Nile, hunting wild animals for food. Writing had not been invented, so people could not record what happened to them. This time is called 'prehistory'. The Egyptians had no kings and did not build villages or towns. Then, about 5000 BC, they began to settle down in villages, building houses from bricks made of sun-baked mud. They began to farm. They tamed wild sheep, goats and cattle and planted crops – barley and a kind of wheat called emmer wheat. They grew flax to make linen for clothes and used clay to make pots.

A traditional house (right). Mud brick is still used for building in Egypt.

Egypt was starting to become a great country. The Egyptians could grow or make most of the things they needed. They traded with other countries to get other things, such as large logs of wood for building, or luxury items such as precious stones, silver, ivory, gold and exotic animals.

By about 3000 BC the Egyptians invented a kind of picture writing, called hieroglyphic writing. They needed to record all the trading they were doing.

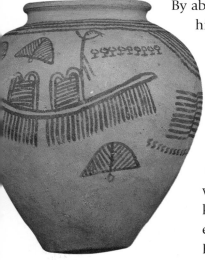

A prehistoric pot with a picture of a boat.

During the prehistoric period Egyptians usually buried the bodies of the dead in the desert. At first, the dead bodies were put into pits dug in the desert sands. The bodies were placed curled up as if they were asleep, and then covered with sand. The sand was so hot it dried all the water out of the bodies and preserved the skin, teeth and bones. These bodies are called sand-dried mummies. The ancient Egyptians believed that after they died their spirits would travel through the underworld to another place. Here they would live again in an Afterlife. The Afterlife was similar to the Egypt they knew, but much better. When the spirit reached the Afterlife it needed to enter a body. This is why the Egyptians made mummies or preserved bodies. Experts think the Egyptians believed in the Afterlife even at this early time because the dead were given jewellery, linen cloth and pots of food to take with them on their journey to the next world.

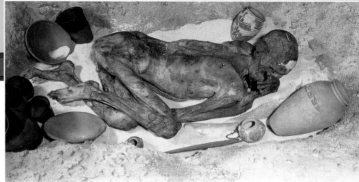

A prehistoric man, whose body was dried in the sand.

A later burial with the body wrapped in mats. Only the bones and some skin are preserved.

Den, an early king of Egypt, attacking his enemies.

Around 3000 BC, the Egyptians began to cover their burial pits with a platform made of mud brick. The pits were now tombs. These tombs were shaped like the rectangular benches outside modern Egyptian houses. The Arabic word for these benches is *mastaba*, so the tombs are called mastaba tombs. We know that, by this time, Egypt was ruled by its first kings. The kings were rich and could afford to build a more elaborate kind of tomb – the pyramid.

A modern house with a mastaba bench.

A mastaba tomb near the Giza pyramids.

A REVOLUTIONARY NEW TOMB

About 4,500 years ago, around 2650 BC, a king called Djoser decided to build a new type of tomb for himself. This tomb is now called the Step Pyramid.

The Step Pyramid and the complex of buildings nearby.

The Step Pyramid was the first major building in the world to be built entirely of stone. Before this time, buildings were made of mud bricks. It was very easy for builders to find mud along the banks of the River Nile, but it was not so easy for them to get good stone. Djoser had to bring two types of stone to Saqqara. Granite came from Aswan, hundreds of miles away in the far south of Egypt. Limestone came to the site from the other side of the Nile. Only a powerful king could have organized such an unusual, expensive and complicated project.

Who was Djoser? Who helped him build his pyramid?

Djoser
the king who mined for make-up

A statue of King Djoser, found at Saqqara.

Djoser's father, Khasekhemwy, had been a successful ruler. Khasekhemwy stopped the fighting between different peoples in northern and southern Egypt and made Egypt a strong and unified country. Djoser's mother was Queen Nemathap. When they died, Khasekhemwy and Nemathap were buried at a place called Abydos, but Djoser decided that his tomb would be at Saqqara, near the royal capital city of Memphis where he lived.

Djoser was a very successful king, and ruled Egypt for nineteen years. Most people today only remember him for building the Step Pyramid, but he did other great things for Egypt. He opened up mines to find copper for tools, turquoise for jewellery and minerals for eye make-up. He traded with other countries for goods Egypt needed, such as wood for ships. He created hundreds of jobs for scribes and record-keepers, potters and rope-makers. Egypt's farmers also flourished.

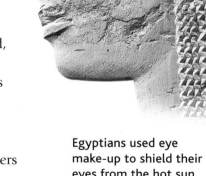

Egyptians used eye make-up to shield their eyes from the hot sun.

Imhotep   *the builder of the Step Pyramid*

Djoser's Step Pyramid was designed by a very wise and clever man called Imhotep. Imhotep had many important titles, which tell us the kinds of work he did. First, he was a Vizier – something like a British Prime Minister or an American Vice-President. The Vizier helped the king run the country. Imhotep was also known as the 'Great Seer of Re'. This means he was a High Priest who could 'see' and speak for the god Re. He was also a healer and was often associated with medicine, but he is most famous for being an architect. Imhotep was remembered in Egyptian history for thousands of years and even worshipped as a god.

Statue of Imhotep, the architect of the Step Pyramid. He is dressed as a priest.

THE SAQQARA COMPLEX

The Step Pyramid, like most other Egyptian pyramids, does not stand all by itself. It is part of a 'complex' or group of buildings.

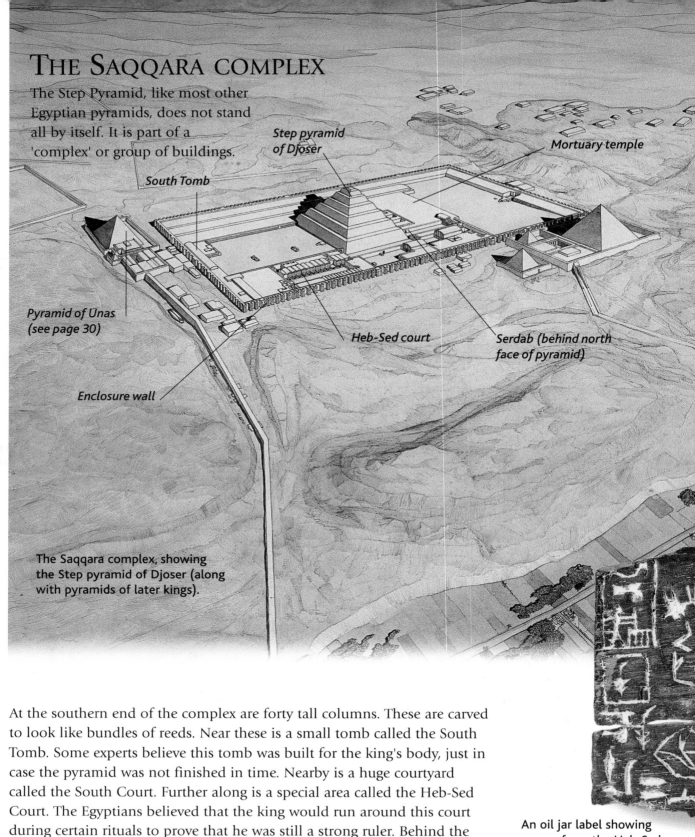

Step pyramid of Djoser

Mortuary temple

South Tomb

Pyramid of Unas (see page 30)

Heb-Sed court

Serdab (behind north face of pyramid)

Enclosure wall

The Saqqara complex, showing the Step pyramid of Djoser (along with pyramids of later kings).

At the southern end of the complex are forty tall columns. These are carved to look like bundles of reeds. Near these is a small tomb called the South Tomb. Some experts believe this tomb was built for the king's body, just in case the pyramid was not finished in time. Nearby is a huge courtyard called the South Court. Further along is a special area called the Heb-Sed Court. The Egyptians believed that the king would run around this court during certain rituals to prove that he was still a strong ruler. Behind the pyramid is Djoser's mortuary temple. This temple was where the embalmers mummified the dead king's body before it was taken into the pyramid.

An oil jar label showing scenes from the Heb-Sed festival of Den, a very early king of Egypt.

Mastaba tombs

The king
running at his
jubilee festival.

The king
seated in a
kiosk.

Near the pyramid was a small but very special building called a *serdab*. Inside this dark room sits a statue of Djoser, wearing a wig, a cloak and a false beard. The statue stares through two eye-holes in the wall. The Egyptians believed that if the king's mummy was destroyed, his spirit could live in this statue.

The serdab of Djoser, with two eye-holes for the statue to look through.

Today, the Step Pyramid is still visible from miles away.

BUILDING THE STEP PYRAMID

The Step Pyramid, the tomb where the king's mummy was buried, was the most important building in the complex. Imhotep made the Step Pyramid look like a giant staircase, so the spirit of his king could get nearer to the sun. He was also in charge of all the builders, making sure they did their work properly.

The base of the Step Pyramid is a rectangular shape, because it copied the shape of a mastaba tomb. Most of the Step Pyramid was built of blocks of limestone. These blocks were cut in local quarries and were not of the best quality. It was all right to use poorer quality limestone for the inside of the pyramid, because nobody would see it.

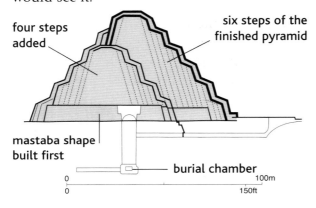

four steps added

six steps of the finished pyramid

mastaba shape built first

burial chamber

0   100m
0   150ft

The first layer of limestone blocks was laid on the ground. It looked like a mastaba tomb. Then another slightly smaller layer of limestone blocks was put on top of this. Another four layers of blocks were put on top, each one smaller than the one before. There are six layers in all.

When the pyramid was finished, good-quality white limestone was used to cover the outside. When the rays of the sun hit the white limestone, the pyramid shone. It could be seen from miles away!

Tura quarry, the source of good-quality white limestone. The quarry is still used today.

Today the outer coating has gone and you can see the inner blocks forming the six steps of Djoser's pyramid.

Inside the pyramid were many corridors and rooms. These corridors were decorated with pictures of the king carved in the stone. When the king was alive he had a private palace so he needed to have the same when he was dead. Several of his private rooms were lined with beautiful blue tiles. The colour may have reminded the dead king of the River Nile and the fields nearby.

A turquoise blue tile from inside the Step Pyramid.

Beneath the pyramid was the burial chamber. This was where the priests hid the mummy of Djoser. It was the most important place in the pyramid. The burial chamber was lined with the second type of stone, granite. This very hard stone was cut in quarries in Aswan, in the south of Egypt. It was brought up the river on boats and then thousands of men dragged it across the land on sledges. Luckily, Djoser had plenty of men and oxen to pull these heavy sledges.

Large blocks of stone were pulled along on wooden sledges like this one.

Djoser's mummy has never been found. Parts of at least one mummy were found in the pyramid, but we do not know if any of them belonged to the great king himself. Luckily for Djoser, the king's spirit could live inside the statue of the king sitting inside its dark serdab room.

THE FIRST TRUE PYRAMIDS

After Djoser, several kings tried to build pyramids, but the next really great pyramid builder was a king called Sneferu. His name means 'to make beautiful'. Sneferu became king when he was a young man and he lived for many years so he had plenty of time to build his pyramid. In fact, he built three pyramids in two different places in Egypt: one at Meidum and two at Dashur.

Sneferu
soldiers, slaves and ships

Experts think that Sneferu was the son of King Huni. Sneferu married Hetepheres. They had a son called Khufu, who is famous for building the Great Pyramid at Giza.

Sneferu became king about 2613 BC. Stories about Sneferu tell us that he was a good and wise king. Information written inside his pyramids suggests that he may have ruled for up to fifty years.

When Sneferu became king, Egypt was a strong country. A king could only build pyramids if he was a successful ruler and his country was wealthy. How did Sneferu make his country wealthy? He sent soldiers down to the south of Egypt into a land called Nubia. Nowadays, this part of Africa is called Sudan. The soldiers traded for things that Egypt needed. They also brought back thousands of cattle and prisoners from Nubia. These prisoners helped to build the king's pyramids.

A limestone block carved with Sneferu's name in hieroglyphs.

A statue of King Sneferu.

Sneferu also sent soldiers to protect the trade routes to the copper mines in Egypt. One area, Sinai, was very important to the ancient Egyptians as it was famous for its turquoise mines. In later years the turquoise miners worshipped Sneferu as a god, because they were so grateful to him for protecting them.

A gold box and bracelets belonging to Queen Hetepheres.

Sneferu built many ships and sent them on trading voyages to the Lebanon, Nubia and Sinai. During his reign the Nile floods never failed. Harvests were good, so everyone had plenty of food and the country was rich.

This painting shows Nubians bringing gold to Egypt.

THE MEIDUM PYRAMID

Sneferu built his first pyramid at Meidum, near the capital city at Memphis. Sneferu's Vizier was Nefermaat, one of his sons. Nefermaat was probably the architect who designed Sneferu's pyramids. He planned the Meidum pyramid with a square base, not rectangular like Djoser's Step Pyramid.

The plan shows something very interesting about this pyramid. It was built in stages. Sneferu started to build the pyramid with seven steps. He covered these with a layer of smooth, slippery limestone. Later, he built another pyramid over the first one, making it into eight steps. This was also covered with a smooth layer of limestone. Experts think it took about fourteen years for the workmen to build these two stages.

The causeway (road) leading to the Meidum Pyramid.

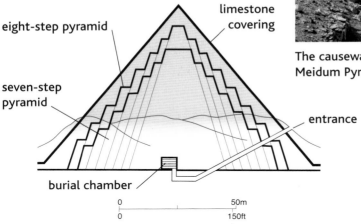

eight-step pyramid

limestone covering

seven-step pyramid

entrance

burial chamber

| 0 | 50m |
| 0 | 150ft |

Then Sneferu stopped building it. He had decided to move to another place and build other pyramids. Years later he returned to the pyramid at Meidum and added more stone. This made it into a true pyramid with smooth sides.

Over the years the two layers of slippery limestone slid downwards, pulling down some of the blocks underneath. Nowadays, there are only three steps of the original pyramid left. The rest lies around in piles on the ground.

The burial chamber is at the ground level of the pyramid. This is where the priests should have put the king's body, but experts think he was buried somewhere else. This was the first time the Egyptians built a burial chamber with a roof that was 'corbelled' (in a stepped arch shape).

The Meidum complex and other tombs

The Meidum pyramid stood in a complex of buildings. There was a mortuary temple, where the priests prayed for the spirit of the dead king. There was a valley temple built near the River Nile. Here, the king's body would be received by priests and prepared for burial. A long causeway (a specially-built road) connected the valley temple to the main pyramid area. Originally a wall went around the complex, but not much of it is left today.

Outside this wall were the tombs of Sneferu's family. One mastaba tomb belonged to Sneferu's son Nefermaat and his wife Atet. This tomb has beautiful artwork painted on the walls. There are men building a boat and a child playing with a monkey. The most famous scene shows a group of Egyptian geese.

Painting of Egyptian geese in the tomb of Nefermaat and Atet.

In the tomb of another son, Rahotep, archaeologists found statues of him and his wife Nofret. They are wearing white linen, colourful jewellery and wigs. The eyes in the statues are made of highly-polished rock crystal, with iris and pupil shown in paint. They look very life-like. The statues of Rahotep and Nofret are two of the most beautiful ever found in Egypt.

Double statue of Sneferu's son Rahotep and his wife Nofret.

This carving from Rahotep's tomb shows an offering table with food for the afterlife.

THE 'BENT' PYRAMID

Sneferu did not build his next two pyramids at Meidum but at Dashur, close to Egypt's capital city, Memphis. Experts think he probably wanted to be buried nearer to the capital.

This photograph of the Bent Pyramid shows why it got its name. Halfway up the sides of the pyramid it changes shape and looks bent. The architects realized they were building the pyramid too steeply, so they changed the angle. This pyramid was made of much larger blocks of limestone than the earlier pyramids. These were much more difficult to lift into place. Again, these blocks were covered with good quality smooth limestone. A lot of this outer casing is still there.

The Bent Pyramid has two separate burial chambers. Some experts think one chamber was for the king's mummy and the second for his wife's. Other experts think that the second chamber was for the king's spirit to live in.

The pyramid was not alone. It had mortuary and valley temples. In the courtyard outside were six stone statues of Sneferu. People worshipped these statues.

Another of Sneferu's sons, Prince Kanefer, was buried in a cemetery quite near the Bent Pyramid. Like his brothers Nefermaat and Rahotep, Kanefer died before his father.

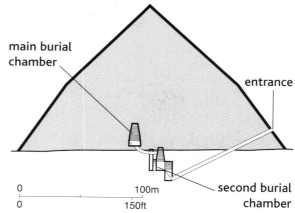

main burial chamber

entrance

second burial chamber

0   100m
0   150ft

THE RED PYRAMID

Sneferu built a second pyramid at Dashur. Perhaps he was disappointed with the shape of the Bent Pyramid and decided to have another go at pyramid building. So he built the Red Pyramid, which is also known as the 'Shining Pyramid'.

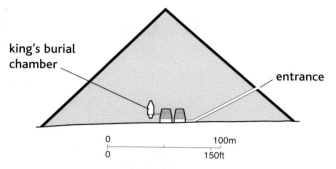

king's burial chamber

entrance

```
0                    100m
0                    150ft
```

Inside the Red Pyramid's burial chamber: can you see the door at the bottom right-hand side of the room?

The Red Pyramid is a true pyramid shape. Its sides slope very gently – it is the flattest of all Egypt's pyramids. Why is it called the Red Pyramid? Originally, it had a covering of smooth white limestone like other pyramids, but this was stolen. It was easy for robbers to climb up the pyramid and remove the limestone because the pyramid's sides were so flat. The stone underneath is a reddish colour because it contains a mineral called iron oxide.

The Red Pyramid has one burial chamber. It is just above ground level, towards the middle of the pyramid. Archaeologists think Sneferu wanted to be buried here. Some human remains – a skull, pieces of ribs, a finger and part of a hip bone – were found in the burial chamber. These belonged to a middle-aged man and may be all that is left of the great pyramid builder, King Sneferu.

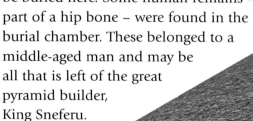

The Red Pyramid, with its long sloping sides.

THE GIZA PYRAMIDS

Three large pyramids rise up out of the desert at Giza. They are probably the most famous monuments from ancient Egypt. They were built by three kings from the Fourth Dynasty, a family who ruled Egypt over 4,000 years ago. At that time, the pyramids and their surrounding temples and smaller buildings stood in the empty desert. Today the modern city of Cairo has spread up close to the site.

The Egyptian names of the three kings who built these pyramids were Khufu, Khafre and Menkaure. Sometimes they are called by Greek names: Cheops, Chephren and Mycerinus. This is because Greek people who visited Egypt centuries after the pyramids were built found Egyptian names difficult to say, so they gave each king a Greek-sounding name.

Tourists have visited Giza for hundreds of years. These are Victorian tourists near Khufu's Great Pyramid.

The three main pyramids were royal tombs, and the kings were buried inside the pyramids when they died. Nearby, there are smaller pyramids, tombs and graves for members of the royal family and important people who worked for the kings. Today, only a few of these smaller pyramids are still standing.

Standing in the desert: the Giza pyramids (left to right: Menkaure, Khafre, Khufu).

A block of stone from Giza with Khufu's name in hieroglyphs.

Dr Zahi Hawass is in charge of antiquities in Egypt. Here he is studying his plans of the Giza pyramids.

The wooden boat which took Khufu's mummy to his pyramid tomb.

KHUFU'S BOATS

Archaeologists found seven pits around Khufu's pyramid. Five of the pits were empty. In 1954, archaeologists were surprised and excited to find that the sixth pit contained an enormous cedar-wood boat buried deep in the sand. They realized that this was the boat which had carried the mummy of King Khufu across the Nile to be buried in his pyramid. Special cameras show that there is another boat waiting to be discovered in the seventh pit.

THE GREAT PYRAMID OF KHUFU

The Great Pyramid was built by King Khufu around 2600 BC. It is 137 m (460 ft) tall and was made of about 2,300,000 blocks of limestone, plus a covering of smooth white limestone. Most of the white covering has now disappeared. A smaller pyramid made of gold may have stood on the top. The white limestone and gold would have shone dazzlingly bright in the Egyptian sun. This pyramid is the biggest in Egypt and is the only one of the Seven Wonders of the Ancient World still standing.

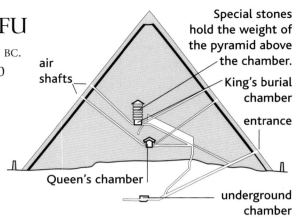

Special stones hold the weight of the pyramid above the chamber.

air shafts

King's burial chamber

entrance

Queen's chamber

underground chamber

```
0                    100m
0                    150ft
```

Khufu *a mystery king*

Khufu became king of Egypt about 2589 BC. His father was the great pyramid builder Sneferu and his mother was Hetepheres.

There is just one statue of King Khufu to give us an idea of what he looked like. The statue is made of ivory and is only 7.5 cm (3 in) tall. It shows the king seated on his throne and looking very confident.

Some of the Greek authors wrote that Khufu was a bad person. They said he spent all of Egypt's money and made his people work in terrible conditions. They said he executed hundreds of people. But nobody knows the truth. We have no information about Khufu written down by people who knew him when he was alive. What we do know is that he built one of the most famous monuments in the world.

This tiny statue is the only surviving image of King Khufu.

Khufu's architect

The architect of the Great Pyramid was called Hemon. He was Khufu's nephew, the son of Khufu's brother Nefermaat. Hemon was also Khufu's Vizier, so he was very powerful. His statue shows him as a large, plump man. This means he was very successful in his job and that he could afford plenty of food.

Inside the Great Pyramid

The real entrance to the pyramid is 15 m (49 ft) above ground, but today tourists visiting the Great Pyramid go in through another entrance made lower down in modern times.

From the entrance, you walk down a steep passage to the king's original burial chamber under the pyramid. It was never finished so the king was not buried there. Now walk along another steep passage going upwards. You will enter a room called the Queen's Chamber, but the queen was not buried there. Carry on walking upwards and enter the wonderful Grand Gallery. Here the walls are 8 m (26 ft) high. This long gallery leads to the middle of the pyramid where Khufu was buried in a room known as the King's Chamber. Here there is a huge red granite sarcophagus, or stone coffin. Khufu's mummy is no longer there but his name is written in red paint on the ceiling above.

In 1993 a little tank-shaped robot explored narrow shafts in the pyramid. The robot, now in the British Museum, found a tiny doorway but the shafts are much too small for people to use. No one knows what they were built for.

The original arched entrance to the Great Pyramid and, below it, the entrance used by modern visitors.

The empty sarcophagus of Khufu inside the King's Chamber.

The robot which explored the long, narrow shafts of the Great Pyramid in 1993.

Pyramids of the Queens

Near the Great Pyramid are three smaller pyramids known as the Queens' pyramids. One was for Khufu's sister, Henutsen. The middle pyramid was for Meretetes, a queen who seems to have lived for a very long time. The third pyramid probably belonged to Queen Hetepheres, Khufu's mother. In 1925, some archaeologists found a deep shaft near this pyramid. At the bottom of the shaft were many items belonging to Hetepheres: pottery, jewellery, furniture and a sedan (or carrying) chair with her name on it. There was an alabaster canopic chest with the queen's mummified organs still inside. Best of all, there was her beautiful alabaster sarcophagus but, when it was opened, the mummy of Hetepheres was not inside.

The splendid wooden carrying-chair of Queen Hetepheres.

The three smaller pyramids belonged to the ladies in Khufu's family.

THE PYRAMID OF KHAFRE

Khafre became king about 2558 BC. Khafre's pyramid is smaller than Khufu's pyramid, but it is built on higher ground, so it looks taller. It was built using about 1,500,000 limestone blocks. It is the only pyramid at Giza on which it's still possible to see some of the original white, smooth limestone covering.

Khafre's pyramid, with some of the original limestone casing remaining near the top, and (below) a statue of Khafre.

Khafre *a wealthy king*

When King Khufu died Khafre became king. Khafre's mother was Henutsen. He was married to two queens, Khamerernebty I and Meresankh. Khamerernebty's son was Menkaure, who became king after his father.

This magnificent statue of Khafre is made of black diorite, a hard stone brought from Nubia. Khafre is seated and wears a false beard, the sign of a king. His face looks calm and intelligent. Behind Khafre sits the god Horus in the form of a falcon. The bird's wings are folded around the king to protect him. This protection worked because Khafre was king for twenty-five successful years. Egypt was a wealthy country during his reign.

Inside Khafre's pyramid

Outside the pyramid is a large courtyard. It was surrounded by a high wall, but today much of this is missing – only 2 m (6 ft 6 in) remains. In Greek and Roman times people thought this pyramid was solid, with no rooms inside and no entrance. Later adventurers found out the truth.

In 1818, an Italian adventurer, Giovanni Belzoni, decided to discover the secrets of this pyramid. He thought he would be the first person inside this mysterious place since it had been sealed up, but he was wrong. When he entered the pyramid, he found some Arabic writing from the 12th century on a wall in the burial chamber. It said that King Ali Mohammed had opened up the tomb – 600 years before! Belzoni realized he was not the first inside the pyramid. He was disappointed so he also scratched his name, and the date, on the same wall in enormous letters.

Portrait of Belzoni, wearing Arabic clothing,

Belzoni's writing inside the pyramid. It means 'discovered by G. Belzoni'.

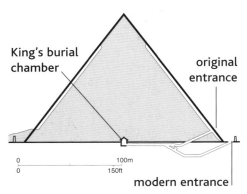

King's burial chamber

original entrance

modern entrance

0   100m
0   150ft

Statues of the women in Queen Meresankh's family stand at the back of her mastaba tomb.

Inside the pyramid he found there were two entrances. One passage ran downwards into the burial chamber. Here Belzoni found a pit in the floor of the chamber. This was to hold the canopic jars in which the king's internal organs were stored. Then he found Khafre's sarcophagus, made from hard, black granite. The mummy of the king was not there but the sarcophagus was not empty. The bones of a bull were in it – some experts think the bones were an offering made to the king a long time after his mummy was stolen.

There are no pyramids for Khafre's wife and female relatives but his wife, Meresankh III, is buried in a mastaba tomb nearby. The tomb contains ten statues of the queen and her female relatives. The mummy of Queen Meresankh was found in a black granite sarcophagus in her burial chamber.

THE GREAT SPHINX

Crouching near the pyramids at Giza is the gigantic statue of a lion with a human head. It is 72 m (236 ft) long and 20 m (65 ft 6 in) tall and is the largest statue in Egypt. It is called the Sphinx and it was also built by Khafre.

The Great Sphinx crouches beside Khafre's pyramid.

A fragment of the Sphinx's broken-off beard, now in the British Museum.

A statue of King Thutmose IV offering gifts to the gods.

The statue looks as if it is guarding the pyramids. Centuries after the time of Khafre, the Greeks named it the Sphinx because it reminded them of similar statues in their home country.

Many people believe the Sphinx's face is modelled on the king's face. At one time the Sphinx had a stone plaited beard but now it has fallen off.

An Egyptian story tells us that many years later a young prince named Thutmose visited the Sphinx. Thutmose fell asleep by the statue. He dreamt that the sun god told him to clean and repair the Sphinx. In exchange he would become king of Egypt. Thutmose did as he was asked and even painted the Sphinx in bright red, blue and yellow colours. He did become king, as Thutmose IV.

The Pyramid of Menkaure

Menkaure became king when his father Khafre died, about 2532 BC. He ruled Egypt for about twenty-eight years. Menkaure's was the last royal pyramid to be built at Giza.

Menkaure
a king who loved his children

We do not have many records from the time of Menkaure. Writing many centuries later, the Greek writer Herodotus tells us that Menkaure was a good king. The Egyptians loved him because he prayed to the gods and he looked after the temples.

Menkaure was married. His queen was Khamerernebty II. He had several children, and his son Shepseskaf was king after him. Herodotus tells us about the king's grief when one of his young daughters died. The story says she was buried in a gold coffin in the shape of a cow. Another daughter was called Khentkawes.

The pyramid of Menkaure standing in the desert. On the left is one of the smaller pyramids for a female relative.

A statue of Menkaure and his wife Khamerernebty II standing side by side. The black stone statue was once painted in bright colours.

The Third Pyramid of Giza

Menkaure's pyramid was made of two types of stone. The lower part is made of reddish-grey granite, brought up from Aswan in southern Egypt. The upper part is made of white limestone.

Menkaure's pyramid stands 66 m (216 ft) tall. It is the smallest of the three Giza pyramids but is in the best condition. The entrance is 4m (13 ft) above ground and a passage goes down to the burial chamber, which has a curved ceiling. There is a store room attached to it.

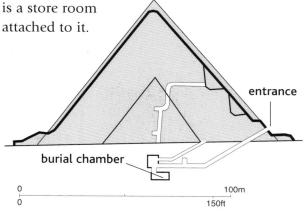

The pyramid is made of granite blocks at the bottom, with limestone blocks for the upper half.

The Queen's Pyramids

Menkaure built three smaller pyramids for the women in his family. Menkaure's name was written in red ochre on the ceiling of one pyramid. In the middle pyramid, which was built for his wife, the body of a young woman was found. Maybe this is Queen Khamerernebty II?

Near Menkaure's pyramid is a large mastaba tomb. The name on the doorway is Khentkawes, one of his daughters. Khentkawes was the mother of two later kings of Egypt. Experts think she ruled Egypt for her sons until they grew up, and for this she was allowed her own royal tomb.

Mastaba tomb.

Lost at sea

In 1837, two Englishmen found a beautiful dark sarcophagus in the burial chamber. Inside this was a wooden coffin with Menkaure's name written on it. Some bones from a male human body were found in another room. People thought this might be Menkaure himself.

In 1838, the sarcophagus and the mummified body were put on separate ships sailing to England. The ship carrying the sarcophagus sank, but the coffin and mummy arrived at the British Museum. Tests on the bones showed that the body could not be King Menkaure. It came from a time hundreds of years later.

These hieroglyphs on the wooden coffin write part of Menkaure's name in an oval 'cartouche'. You can see the whole cartouche on page 28.

THE PYRAMID OF UNAS

The next pyramid was built about two hundred years later, at the end of the Fifth Dynasty. Around 2375 BC King Unas ruled Egypt. (Some people spell his name as Wenis.) Unas, like Djoser and several other kings before him, built his pyramid at Saqqara.

The pyramid of Unas. Today it is not in very good condition.

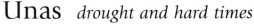

Unas *drought and hard times*

There isn't a great deal of information about Unas as a person. He never tells the names of his parents. He had two wives named Nebet and Khennut. They were buried in mastaba tombs near their husband's pyramid.

At this time in Egypt the weather was changing. The country was becoming much drier, making it more difficult for people to grow food. The Egyptians had problems trading down in the southern part of Egypt. King Unas had to travel south to sort out these troubles. Times were hard and Unas was not as wealthy as some of the earlier kings. This might be why his pyramid is the smallest of all the royal Egyptian pyramids.

Wealthy people were still buried in mastaba tombs in this area. This is a statue of an important man named Mereruka from a later mastaba tomb at Saqqara.

Outside the Unas Pyramid

Some distance away from the pyramid was a valley temple, where the mummy of Unas would lie waiting to be taken up to the pyramid.

Between the valley temple and the entrance hall of the pyramid there is a long causeway. The Unas causeway is very interesting because it has carved pictures, which tell us about how work was done in the Old Kingdom of Egypt. One carving shows how large pieces of stone were moved from one part of the country to another. There are barges, each carrying two tall granite columns to be used to hold up ceilings or decorate courtyards. The barges sail up the river from the granite quarries at Aswan.

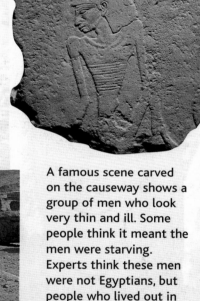

The causeway (road) leading through tall door jambs to the pyramid of Unas.

A famous scene carved on the causeway shows a group of men who look very thin and ill. Some people think it meant the men were starving. Experts think these men were not Egyptians, but people who lived out in the desert without enough to eat.

Some of the carvings show Egyptians fighting their enemies and taking prisoners. There are wild animals such as lions, leopards and giraffes. Other carvings show craftsmen at work. We see goldsmiths making jewellery, plates and bowls and carpenters making wooden objects needed for building the pyramid and for the king's burial.

Carving on the causeway showing carpenters at work.

INSIDE THE UNAS PYRAMID

In the pyramids already described, the entrance is usually quite high above the ground. The pyramid of Unas is different. The entrance opens straight from the courtyard.

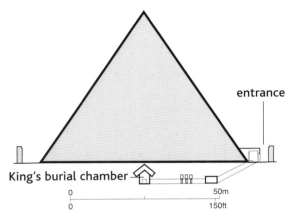

entrance

King's burial chamber

| 0 | | 50m |
| 0 | | 150ft |

From the entrance a passage runs down to a long corridor. It meets an antechamber, the room before the burial chamber. On the left are three store rooms where the priests put food, clothing and other things for the dead king. On the right is the burial chamber.

Archaeologists found a black stone sarcophagus in the burial chamber. The king's canopic chest lay in a pit near the sarcophagus. On the floor they found parts of a human body: an arm and hand, part of a leg bone and parts of a skull. Are these the remains of King Unas? These bones are now in the Cairo Museum.

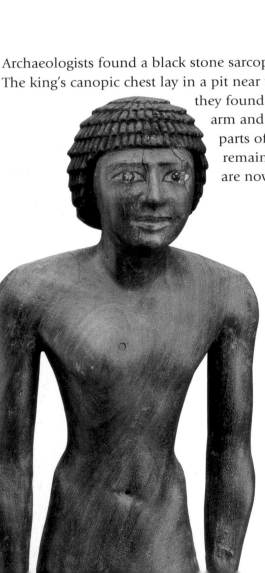

Archaeologists sometimes examine bones to find out if the dead person was a man or woman and if they were old or young. Sometimes the bones show if the person was ill with a disease. This skull and wooden statue were found in the tomb of a lector-priest called Meryrahashetef. Meryrahshetef's teeth are very worn down, possibly from eating bread with grit in it.

The Pyramid Texts

The walls in the burial chamber in the Unas pyramid are striking. Around the sarcophagus the walls are decorated to look like a reed mat. The ceiling is painted dark blue with golden stars. The mummy of Unas would lie in his coffin and look up at the night stars painted above.

On the other walls in the burial chamber there is something very exciting indeed. They are covered in hieroglyphs! These writings are known as the Pyramid Texts and this is the first time hieroglyphic writing appears in a pyramid in ancient Egypt.

The walls were first covered with white alabaster, a stone with a very fine smooth surface. Then long rows of hieroglyphs were carved into the alabaster. These were painted the same blue-green colour used in Djoser's Step Pyramid.

Inside the burial chamber of the Unas pyramid, the walls are covered with magic spells written in hieroglyphs.

The god Osiris.

The Pyramid texts are like magical spells meant to protect the dead king. The spells tell us the story of the king's burial – how his mummified body was taken in a procession from the Valley Temple to the burial chamber inside the pyramid. The texts describe King Unas climbing a ladder to heaven where he will meet the gods. The Egyptians also believed that the king's spirit travelled across the sky every morning to meet the sun-god – this was day-time. At night the mummy of Unas slept in his tomb and talked to Osiris, king of the Afterlife – this was night-time. In this way Unas made sure there were always days and nights in Egypt.

THE LAST ROYAL PYRAMIDS

After Unas, only one or two more kings built pyramids. Then Egypt went through a difficult time. There was disorder in the country, and the kings could not control the different groups trying to get power. For about a hundred years kings stopped building pyramids. About 1991 BC a new and strong family of kings took over Egypt. These kings are known as the 12th Dynasty. Several of them liked the idea of building themselves pyramids.

This family of kings had their capital city near Memphis and built their pyramids in an area of Egypt called the Fayum. This was an oasis area. There was plenty of water so food was grown in large amounts. The Fayum was famous for its fruit trees and for hunting and fishing. Two 12th Dynasty kings built especially interesting pyramids. Their names are Senusret II and Amenemhet III.

Farmers in the Fayum using a water wheel to water their fields.

Senusret II

more food, more farmers

Senusret II became king of Egypt about 1897 BC. He was king for about twenty years. At this time Egypt was a peaceful country. Senusret developed the Fayum area and made it bigger so farmers could grow even more food for the people.

The best hieroglyphs were written during the Twelfth Dynasty. This little building is covered with beautifully-carved pictures and hieroglyphs, like these.

Senusret's pyramid

Like his father and grandfather before him, Senusret built himself a pyramid tomb. He built his pyramid near the modern village of El Lahun and it was the first pyramid to be made using mud-brick.

The middle of the pyramid was made of yellow limestone. A layer of mud-brick was put on top of this and then another layer of limestone. The top half of the pyramid was made entirely of mud-brick. Nowadays, much of the pyramid has collapsed, probably because the mud-brick was not strong enough.

The burial chamber is 16 m (52ft 6in) under ground. It contains an alabaster offering table and a red granite sarcophagus, but this is empty. Unfortunately, robbers got into the tomb. All that is left of Senusret II are some leg bones.

The pyramid of Senusret II. The mud brick has collapsed.

Making mud bricks.

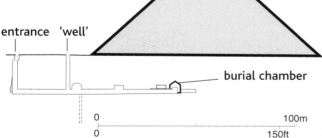

entrance 'well'

burial chamber

0   100m
0   150ft

Pyramid worker's town

Archaeologists have found the old town of El Lahun where the men who built Senusret's pyramid lived. Many of the objects found there tell us about life in the town. There were domestic objects such as combs, mirrors, pottery, perfume pots, tools and even toys. Believe it or not there was even a rat trap made of pottery!

A statue of a *ba*-bird (an image of the spirit of a dead person) and a wooden headrest. Both were found at El Lahun.

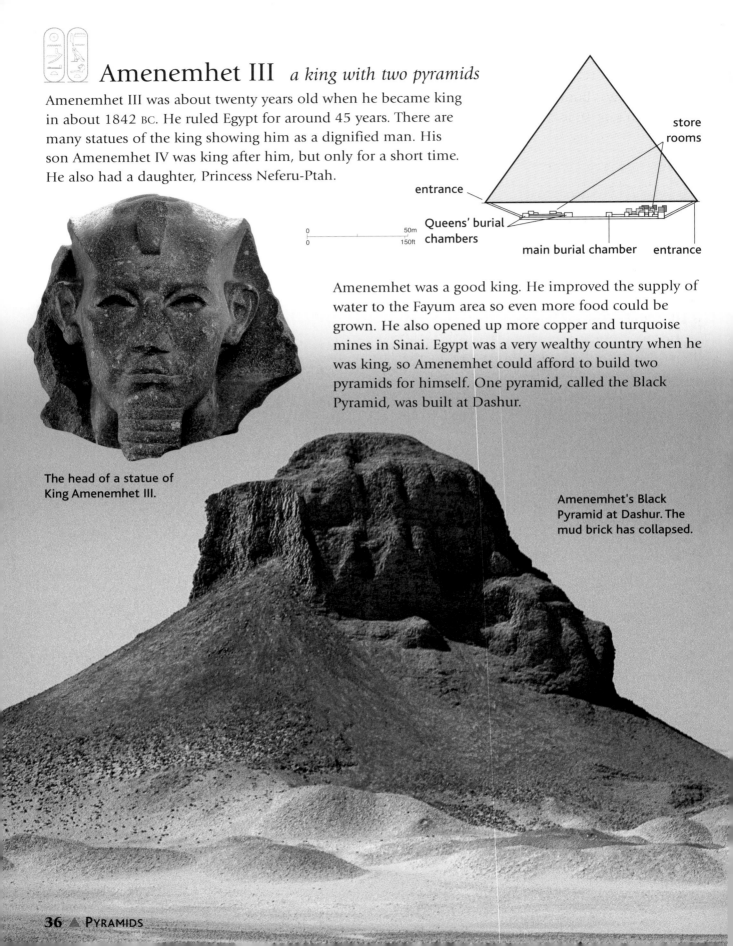

Amenemhet III *a king with two pyramids*

Amenemhet III was about twenty years old when he became king in about 1842 BC. He ruled Egypt for around 45 years. There are many statues of the king showing him as a dignified man. His son Amenemhet IV was king after him, but only for a short time. He also had a daughter, Princess Neferu-Ptah.

store rooms

entrance

Queens' burial chambers

main burial chamber   entrance

0   50m
0   150ft

Amenemhet was a good king. He improved the supply of water to the Fayum area so even more food could be grown. He also opened up more copper and turquoise mines in Sinai. Egypt was a very wealthy country when he was king, so Amenemhet could afford to build two pyramids for himself. One pyramid, called the Black Pyramid, was built at Dashur.

The head of a statue of King Amenemhet III.

Amenemhet's Black Pyramid at Dashur. The mud brick has collapsed.

The Hawara Pyramid

Amenemhet was buried in his other pyramid, which he had built at Hawara. This pyramid may have been named after Sobek, the crocodile-god of the Fayum area.

The pyramid was almost 60 m (197 ft) high. It was made entirely of mud brick and then covered with limestone. The king's burial chamber is in the middle of the pyramid. It is very unusual. The room is actually made from a single piece of quartzite stone, hollowed out like a big box without a lid. It was sealed with a single roofing slab weighing about 46 tonnes (50 tons). Two stone coffins and two chests for canopic jars were found inside this stone room. The large coffin was for Amenemhet. Interestingly, the smaller one was for his daughter Neferu-Ptah. The English Egyptologist Flinders Petrie found bones inside the stone coffins.

The archaeologist Flinders Petrie (who worked in Egypt from 1881 to 1942). He worked in many of Egypt's pyramids.

Amenemhet was buried in this pyramid at Hawara. Now only the mud brick remains.

Outside the Hawara pyramid was a temple, which the Greek writer Herodotus visited. There were so many courtyards, rooms and corridors inside that Herodotus called it the Labyrinth after a famous building at Knossos in Crete. The priests told Herodotus that kings of Egypt were buried there with the mummies of crocodiles, who were worshipped in the Fayum. Experts do not know if this was true.

burial chamber sunk into the ground

entrance

0   50m
0   150ft

Amenemhet III was the last powerful ruler of the Middle Kingdom. It was two hundred years before another great pyramid was built, during the New Kingdom period of Egyptian history.

People who lived in the Fayum area worshipped the crocodile god Sobek. Crocodiles lived in special pools and were mummified when they died.

AHMOSE I AT ABYDOS

Ahmose became king about 1570 BC. He was the first king of the 18th Dynasty, during the New Kingdom period. It was a difficult time in Egypt's history. The Hyksos, foreign peoples from Palestine, had taken over Egypt. Ahmose's father and brother had been killed in battles with the Hyksos. Ahmose was only a young boy when he became king, so his mother, Queen Aahotep, helped him rule the country until he was older. She was a clever and powerful woman.

When he was older Ahmose worked hard as king and finally pushed the Hyksos out of his country. Egypt started trading again and quarries and mines were opened. Egypt once again was a rich country so Ahmose could afford to build a pyramid.

32191.

Shabti, or servant figure, from Ahmose's burial.

Mummy of King Seqenenre, the father of Ahmose. Both men fought the enemy Hyksos.

The Hidden Mummy

The mummified body of King Ahmose, with linen in the eye sockets.

Ahmose built his pyramid at Abydos. It was built as a tomb, but his body was not found there. His mummy was actually found in 1881 in a secret hiding place in Thebes. Many years after Ahmose's death a group of priests moved his mummy, and the mummies of many other kings, and hid them. This was because they were worried that the mummies would be damaged by robbers. Today, the mummy of Ahmose is in the Egyptian Museum in Cairo.

The Last Royal Pyramid

Ahmose's pyramid at Abydos is the last known pyramid built by an Egyptian king. Like earlier pyramids this one was also part of a complex of buildings. It was originally about 49.5 m (162 ft) high and had very steep sides. The photograph shows that the pyramid has almost completely collapsed.

The remains of Ahmose's pyramid.

Ahmose loved and admired his grandmother Queen Tetisherit, so one of the other buildings in the complex was a small shrine to remember her. Near his own pyramid Ahmose also built a small temple for his wife, Ahmose-Nefertary.

Archaeologists found pieces of carved and painted stone at Abydos. These told the story of how Ahmose fought his enemies the Hyksos people.

Nowadays Ahmose's pyramid is not in very good condition. This is because the middle part of it was made of mud brick. The outside was covered with layers of plaster and slabs of stone and over many centuries these layers fell off. Then the stone casing fell off. It does not look very impressive now, but it is the very last royal pyramid of Egypt!

Painting of Queen Ahmose-Nefertary, the wife of Ahmose.

How the pyramids were built

The pyramids of Egypt, especially the Giza pyramids, have been more studied than any other buildings in the world.

King's choice

The king chose the place where his pyramid would be built. The king and his architect decided on the design of the pyramid: how tall, how wide, and how steep the sides would be. Then the architect did the mathematical calculations for the design.

The ancient Egyptians believed that the stars influenced their lives, so astronomers were very important. Astronomers decided which way the pyramids should face to line up with favourable stars.

The Rhind mathematical papyrus in the British Museum shows us that the ancient Egyptians studied mathematics.

Building begins

Stakes were hammered into the ground by the architect's assistants after a special ceremony, in which the king hammered in the first stake. First, all the underground chambers were built and then the core, or middle, of the pyramid. As the core grew, the workmen built into it the chambers and passageways planned by the architect.

Getting and preparing thousands of stone blocks was a difficult task. Rough blocks of stone were brought up the river Nile on flat boats called barges. The stones were dragged on sledges from the barges to the pyramid site, where they were smoothed.

We do not know how the Egyptians actually built their pyramids. Egyptologists have different ideas about this. These diagrams show three possible ways of building a pyramid.

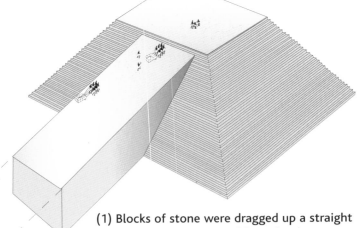

(1) Blocks of stone were dragged up a straight mud ramp. The ramp would need to be very, very long, otherwise it would be too steep. Some experts do not think this is practical.

Not slaves

The ancient Greek writer Herodotus claimed the Great Pyramid was built by slaves, but this is not true. Many of the workers were really farmers. There were certain times of the year when farmers had to wait for their crops to grow. They had nothing to do at this time, so they went to work for the king on building projects.

A baby pyramid like this, called a pyramidion, was placed on the very top of a pyramid.

There were some professional builders in Egypt - stonemasons, carpenters and artists. When they died, the professional builders were buried in a special workmen's cemetery near the Giza pyramids. They were buried in family groups. This proves that they were not slaves. There may be workers' cemeteries which have not yet been found near the other pyramids.

Perfect fit

Nobody knows exactly how the Egyptians built these huge monuments. The stones may have been dragged up a mud ramp built around the pyramid, and then levered into place. The blocks fit together so well that you cannot even get a knife-blade between them.

A small pyramid, or pyramidion, was put on the top of the pyramid. Sometimes it was made of gold. Finally, pure white limestone was brought across the river from the Tura quarries, and placed over the blocks to make the sides of the pyramid beautiful and smooth.

The pyramid complex

While the pyramid was being built, workmen were also building the causeway, temples, storerooms and tombs for the kings' family. All these buildings made up the pyramid complex.

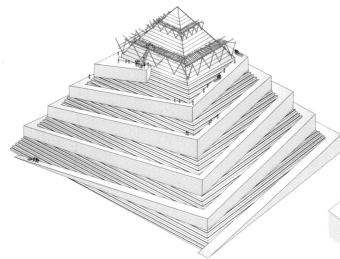

(2) Blocks of stone were dragged up a mud ramp built round and round the pyramid.

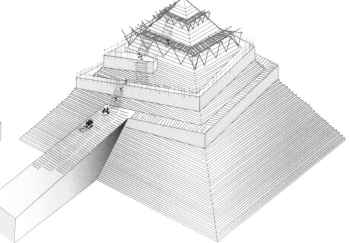

(3) Blocks of stone were dragged up a short, straight mud ramp and then onto a ramp going around the top parts of the pyramid. This combines ideas 1 and 2.

NON-ROYAL PYRAMIDS IN EGYPT

Not all pyramids in Egypt belonged to a king or his family. Some small pyramids actually belonged to ordinary people. These people were artists, stone-masons, sculptors and carpenters. They built the tombs of pharaohs such as Rameses II in the Valley of the Kings.

Every day the craftsmen followed these paths, around the pyramid-shaped mountain called Meret Seger, to reach the Valley of the Kings.

These craftsmen lived in a special village, called Deir el-Medina, high up in the hills. There is not much information about villages from ancient Egypt because very few of them have survived. Deir el-Medina did survive so it is a very important place. Archaeologists found a great deal of written information in this village. Most of it was written on pieces of limestone and pottery, called ostraca. The ostraca tell a great deal about how ordinary Egyptian people lived, the jobs they did and sometimes even their excuses for not going to work! The workers were paid their wages in beer, meat and other things they needed. Once they even went on strike and refused to work because their 'wages' had not arrived.

Statue of King Rameses II.

The remains of the ancient Deir el-Medina village.

Modern mud-brick houses in an Egyptian village.

Buried in style

When the workmen died they were buried in a cemetery near their village. Members of a family were all buried close to one another, in groups. Many of the chief workmen had beautifully decorated tombs. Some had a small mud-brick pyramid placed on top. Many of these tombs have better painted decorations and are in better condition than some of the royal tombs. This is because the chief workmen were clever enough to keep back some of the paint and materials from the royal tombs to use in their own tombs. Also, because the workmen's tombs were smaller they were less likely to be damaged. The royal tombs in the Valley of the Kings were large so, when they were opened in modern times, sand, salt and wind got into them and destroyed many of the wall paintings. Because the workmen's tombs were much smaller, this didn't happen to them.

Small pyramid on top of a chief craftsman's tomb at Deir el-Medina.

This stele (tombstone) is from the tomb of Neferhotep, a chief tomb-artist. It shows him praising queen Ahmose-Nefertary and her son King Amenhotep I.

An ancient Egyptian funeral

priest   mourners   mummy   the god Anubis

Scene on a papyrus showing a funeral. The mummy is going into a pyramid-topped tomb.

Funerals were very important in ancient Egypt. Only wealthy people could afford to be mummified. A priest led the funeral procession as the mummy was dragged on a sledge to its tomb. The dead person's family walked in the procession with other mourners. People screamed and cried in their sadness. Ordinary people had much smaller, simpler funerals.

The mummy was put in the tomb with the things he or she had owned in life – furniture, jewellery and food. A Sem-Priest, dressed in the skin of an exotic cat such as a leopard, touched the mummy's mouth with various tools. This was so the mummy could speak when questioned by the gods at judgement time. Then the tomb was closed and the mummy was left to travel to the Afterlife.

PYRAMIDS OUTSIDE EGYPT

When people think of pyramids they usually think of ancient Egypt, but other cultures in the world built pyramid-like structures.

NUBIAN PYRAMIDS

Nubia (modern Sudan) was a country to the south of Egypt. The peoples of Egypt and Nubia were often in contact, sometimes for peaceful trade and sometimes fighting wars. Nubian kings and queens heard about Egyptian pyramids and decided to use the idea for their own burials. The Nubian pyramids were very different from Egyptian ones. They were smaller and their sides were more sharply sloped. Some of the Nubian kings hid their golden treasure in the little pyramidions on top. Some of the walls are carved with images of the Nubian kings and queens.

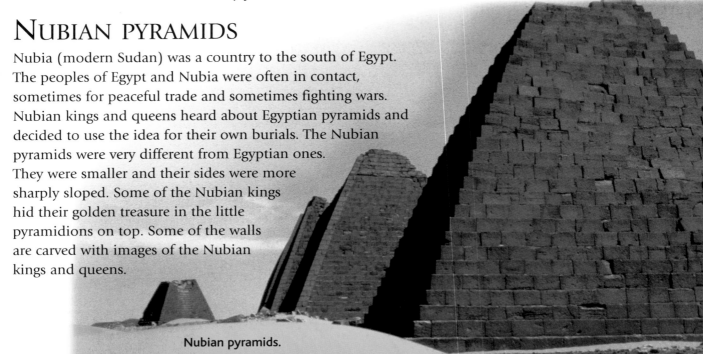

Nubian pyramids.

THE ZIGGURATS OF IRAQ

The ruined ziggurat at Warka.

Further to the east, in the country today called Iraq, other cultures were building up towards the sky. About 4,500 years ago the ancient Sumerians built the famous city of Ur, now in the southern part of Iraq. Archaeologists excavated the remains of the city between 1927 and 1932. They found sixteen royal graves containing spectacular treasure and the remains of a ziggurat. Ziggurats were built of mud-brick and had different stages, very much like the Step Pyramid at Saqqara. Unlike the Saqqara pyramid, ziggurats were not tombs but temples.

Bull's head on a lyre (harp) found in a Sumerian tomb.

THE PYRAMIDS OF MEXICO

In ancient Mexico, the Mayan people built huge pyramid structures, like the Pyramid of the Sun and the Pyramid of the Moon just outside modern Mexico City. These pyramids do not have sloping sides like Egyptian pyramids but are built in stages, rather like large steps. There are two important differences between Egyptian and Mayan pyramids. First, the Mayan pyramids were not tombs. They were temples where Mayan priests performed religious rituals such as prayers and sacrifices. The second difference was that the Mayans could not often go inside their pyramids. Most of the Mayan pyramids were built around a pile of rubble which had no passageways and chambers inside. The Mayans walked up and down their pyramids on the outside.

One Mayan pyramid-temple called the Citadel is in south-eastern Mexico, at a place called Chichén Itzá. The Citadel actually has a secret passageway inside. The passage is dark and narrow and goes into the middle of the pyramid. As you climb up the stairway the stone becomes extremely hot and sweaty! At the end of the passage is a small room where the Mayan priests hid a beautiful red throne shaped like a jaguar.

The Mayan Pyramid of the Sun, which was used as a temple.

A sacred jaguar, painted on a temple wall.

The Citadel pyramid-temple.

ETERNAL PYRAMIDS

For thousands of years people in different parts of the world have made pyramid-shaped buildings. People have always thought the shape very attractive. Modern artists and architects have also been inspired by the pyramids of ancient Egypt.

Mummies' Litul Gizas, a painting by Martin Dexter.

Look around you. Can you spot some examples?

Modern architects have used pyramids in the design of museums, offices and hotels. The Louvre in Paris is one of the most famous museums in the world. It is an old building but at the entrance to the museum there is a modern pyramid made of glass.

The Luxor Hotel, Las Vegas.

The Louvre pyramid.

The Forge shopping centre in Scotland.

The tomb of John Shae Perring, an Englishman who loved exploring Egyptian pyramids.

Buried like an Egyptian

Some modern people have made their gravestones in the shape of a pyramid or have been buried in pyramid tombs.

Laser eyes

The Luxor Hotel at Las Vegas in America is one of the most amazing hotels in the world. The main building is like a huge black pyramid. In front of this black pyramid sits a model of the Sphinx. When it's dark, special lights make the top of the pyramid glow.

The tomb of a Roman called Cestius (first century BC).

A pyramid-shaped tombstone in Kensal Green cemetery, London.

Pyramids are everywhere

You will see pyramids in many places where you might not expect to see them. Look on the back of an American one-dollar bill! Nowadays, there are pyramid-shaped chocolates and teabags. Can you find any more?

US dollar bill.